OLYSLAGER AUTO LIBRARY

# Motorcycles to 1945

compiled by the OLYSLAGER ORGANISATION

edited by Bart H. Vanderveen

FREDERICK WARNE & Co Ltd
London and New York

# THE OLYSLAGER AUTO LIBRARY

This book is one of a growing range of titles on major transport subjects. Titles published so far include:

The Jeep
Cross-Country Cars from 1945
Half-Tracks
Scammell Vehicles
Tank and Transport Vehicles of World War 2
Fire-Fighting Vehicles
Earthmoving Vehicles
Wreckers and Recovery Vehicles
Passenger Vehicles 1893–1940
Buses and Coaches from 1940
Fairground and Circus Transport

American Cars of the 1930s
American Cars of the 1940s
American Cars of the 1950s
American Trucks of the Early Thirties
American Trucks of the Late Thirties

British Cars of the Early Thirties
British Cars of the Late Thirties
British Cars of the Early Forties
British Cars of the Late Forties
British Cars of the Early Fifties
British Cars of the Late Fifties

Motorcycles to 1945

Library of Congress Catalog No. 74-21050

ISBN 0 7232 1825 0

Filmset and printed in Great Britain
by BAS Printers Limited, Wallop, Hampshire
317.974

Although experimental motorized bicycles appeared well before the turn of the century, serious production did not commence until the late 1890s and early 1900s.

The idea was simple: engines existed and so did bicycles—it was only one logical step to take the work out of bicycling. Some people saw the motorcycle as a cheap alternative to the motorcar, while others considered the new machine as exciting transportation: 'straddle the engine, fire it up, release the clutch and you're off and away in a hurry!'.

Ever since its inception there have been two basic types of motorcycles, namely the light motorbicycle which was basically a bicycle with a motor to take over after pedal-starting, and the purpose-built motorcycle. The latter had many derivatives, e.g. sidecar combinations, motortricycles and even tracked cross-country machines. Examples of all these configurations, as produced up to and including the Second World War, are shown in this book.

Over the years there have been hundreds of motorcycle manufacturers, particularly in Western Europe and notably Great Britain. In the late twenties considerably more than half a million motorcycles were registered in Britain, more than in any other country and amounting to about a third of the world's total. Moreover, British motorcycles then were world leaders and their manufacturers scarcely feared foreign competition. Sadly, things have changed dramatically over the last decade or so. Only a few British manufacturers are still in business. In the United States only one, Harley-Davidson, has survived. Germany and other Continental European countries have not fared much better either. Although there is still a market for the products of these remaining few, the Japanese industry has swept the board with machines which the masses wanted, rather than the other way round. That, however, happened after the era which is covered by the following pictorial history which portrays machines of many representative types and sizes, civilian as well as military—with 'humble apologies for the inevitable important omissions'!

Fortunately many old-timers have been preserved by enthusiasts and among the world's leading clubs is the Vintage Motor Cycle Club in Great Britain, whose members own machines of numerous makes and types. In addition, there are many museums, in Britain and abroad, where a great variety of early motorcycles are on display.

**Piet Olyslager MSIA, MSAE, KIVI**

# THE EARLY YEARS

4A Michaux

4B Copeland

4C: Probably the world's first motor (tri)cycle with internal-combustion engine was the Petrol-Cycle, designed in England by Edward Butler and built by Merryweathers of Greenwich. The machine was patented on 14 November 1887 and had a twin-cylinder petrol engine with float-feed carburettor and electric ignition. It was an improved version of an earlier design for which Butler had been granted a patent in 1884.

4D: Gottlieb Daimler's 'single track' machine, patented on 29 August 1885, was the world's first motorbicycle. The machine had outrigger wheels to keep it upright and an air-cooled vertical 264-cc (58 × 100 mm) petrol engine of 0·5 HP at 700 rpm.

4A: Before the internal combustion engine came into being, steam provided the mechanical power to drive most stationary and mobile machinery. It will come as no surprise that steam power was applied also for the propulsion of a two-wheeled *vélocipède*. This model, a French Michaux, was patented by Perreaux on 24 December 1868. It was preceded by an American construction of 1865.

4B: Another early steamer was the machine constructed in 1885 by the American, L. D. Copeland, of Philadelphia. In addition there were several steam-propelled tricycles, produced from the 18th century onwards, but reliable records of these pioneers are virtually non-existent.

4C Butler/Merryweather

4D Daimler

5A Millet

5B Hildebrand & Wolfmüller

5C: Werner's *motocyclette* was one of the few pre-1900 petrol-driven two-wheeled machines built in any quantity. It first appeared in 1897 in France and two years later was licence-produced in England. The French edition had hot-tube ignition but the one made in Coventry featured a battery and coil system. However, the location and excessive weight of the engine made this motorized bicycle (of which several examples have survived) top-heavy and rather difficult to handle.

5D: More a three-wheeled car than a motortricycle, this *voiturette* was first made in LeMans in 1895 by Léon Bollée, a son of the French steam road vehicle pioneer Amédée Bollée. The low-slung tandem two-seater had a 3-HP single-cylinder 650-cc engine with hot-tube ignition and three-speed transmission.

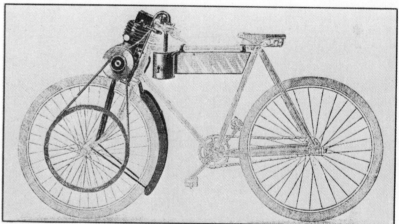

5C Werner

5A: The 1890s saw several more experimental motorbicycles, although tricycles were in the majority. This two-wheeler was a French *bicyclette* of 1892, produced by Millet. It was powered by a five-cylinder rotary engine built in the rear wheel. Several were sold in 1894, named 'La Rue Soleil'.

5B: The German Hildebrand & Wolfmüller had first been conceived in 1892/93 and went into quantity production in Munich in 1894, making it the world's first production motorbicycle. It had a 1488-cc (90 × 117 mm) horizontal twin-cylinder petrol engine of 2½ HP at 240 rpm.

5D Léon Bollée

# THE EARLY YEARS

6A/B: In 1895 the French Count Albert De Dion and his partner Georges Bouton introduced a pedalling tricycle with a modified Daimler engine located behind the rear axle. This reasonably successful machine was produced until 1902 and was copied or licence-produced by several other manufacturers. The engine was a single-cylinder unit of 1¾ HP with automatic inlet valve.

Prior to the production of this motortricycle, the firm, which was founded in 1883, had produced steam-powered vehicles, including a 40-mph steam tricycle in 1887. After the introduction of their petrol engine, many other manufacturers turned to De Dion-Bouton for power units to install in their own vehicles. The firm was also responsible for the De Dion-type axle configuration, which is still used today. This design comprises a dead axle to carry the wheels and the weight of the car and separate universally-jointed drive shafts to transmit the power from the differential to the wheels.

6C: The Beeston motortricycle first appeared in 1897 and was almost a replica of the De Dion-Bouton (*q.v.*). It was made at Beeston in Nottinghamshire by the bicycle manufacturing firm Thomas Humber, which had been established in 1868. Embossed on the tyres are the words 'The Beeston Patent Pneumatic Tyre'. Other products included four-wheeled motorquadricycles.

6B De Dion-Bouton

6A De Dion-Bouton

6C Beeston

7A: Humber's Coventry works also produced motortricycles; an early model is illustrated. Tom Humber began making motorcycles and tricycles in 1896.

7B: Line-up of early Humbers. Nearest the camera is a 1903/04 'forecar' with a passenger seat between the two front wheels. The vehicle had chain drive and the engine was inclined forward, the cylinder doubling up as the forward part of the frame (this design was of Panther/Phelon & Moore origin).

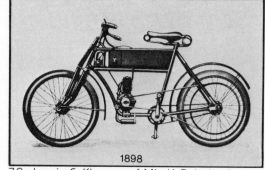

1898

7C: Laurin & Klement of Mladá Boleslav in Czechoslovakia began production of motorcycles in 1898. Shown are the first, a $1\frac{1}{4}$-HP (60 × 65 mm), an 1899 Type B 2-HP (66 × 70 mm), a $2\frac{1}{2}$-HP (75 × 75 mm) of 1901 and a passenger armchair trailer of the same year.

7A Humber

7B Humber

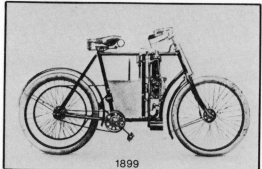

1899

7C Laurin & Klement

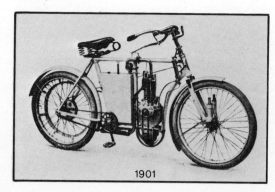

1901

1901

# THE EARLY YEARS

8A Singer

8A : The Singer Cycle Co. Ltd of Coventry, another well-established bicycle manufacturing business, introduced the Singer Motor Wheel in the Autumn of 1900. This motor-wheel, whereby the 2-HP engine was 'sandwiched' between two spoked aluminium discs, had been designed just before the turn of the century by Messrs Perks and Birch and in 1900 Singer had acquired its manufacturing rights. The machine had single-lever control (i.e. a double-action lever, connected with a twisting handle on the handle-bar which either throttled the engine or raised the exhaust valve, as desired), positive drive, magneto ignition, and a combination spray and surface system carburettor. In the 1902 Glenarmuck Hill Trials in Ireland a Singer motortricycle did fastest time, and also faster time than any car under 20 HP in the Gorcot Hill Climb of the Midland Automobile Club.

8B : Singer motortricycle with luggage trunk.

8C : Singer Model 2 Tri-Voiturette of 1902.

# THE EARLY YEARS

9B: Singer motor-wheel model 'for Ladies or Gentlemen'. These bikes were claimed to be good for a road speed of 23 mph and a speed exceeding 40 mph was accomplished on the Crystal Palace track. On 5 July 1902 a similar Singer 'defeated all comers in the Catford Hill-Climbing Competition at Westerham' and on the same occasion this hill was ascended by Mr Perks (*see* 8A) 'without pedal assistance, the chain being detached from the machine'.

9C: Singer 'Chain-Driven Motor Bicycle for Gentlemen'. It was introduced in late 1902 and had basically the same engine as the motor-wheel models. Differences included '. . . free engine for descending hills, complete accessibility to all parts, and a special spring-buffer chain wheel by which remarkably smooth transmission and running are effected. It has been described by independent experts as the cleverest invention pertaining to motorcycles. It is the most silent-running motorbicycle, of its power, at present on the market . . .'

9A: Singer front-drive motortricycle, basically the same as that shown in Fig. 8B, but fitted with wickerwork armchair type passenger seat.

9B Singer

9C Singer

# THE EARLY YEARS

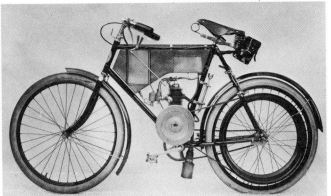

10A FN

10C Laurin & Klement

10D: The first four-cylinder shaft-drive FN appeared in 1905. The 362-cc engine had four tiny 'pots' with bore and stroke of 45 × 57 mm. The 1913/14 edition was a 748-cc (52 × 88 mm) with two-speed gearbox.

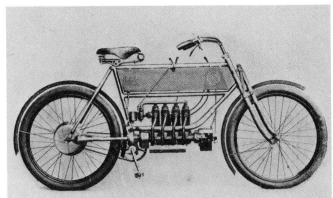

10D FN

10A: The Belgian armaments firm FN (Fabrique Nationale d'Armes de Guerre) of Herstal, near Liège, produced motorcycles of many types from 1902 until the 1960s. The first, shown here, had a two-stroke engine of 133 cc (50 × 68 mm).

10B: The first Hercules motorcycle, made in 1904/05 by the Nürnberger Hercules Werke GmbH of Nuremberg, had a Fafnir engine. The firm had been producing bicycles since 1886.

10C: Laurin & Klement in Czechoslovakia produced V-twins from 1904 and in 1905 introduced a four-in-line. Shown are a 1904 two-cylinder 8 HP (90 × 90 mm) 'pacemaker', used to lead racing-cyclists and produced by various firms in virtually the same form for many years, and a 1905 water-cooled 5 HP (75 × 92 mm) touring model, which was also available with air-cooled cylinders.

10E: A beautifully-restored and preserved Royal Enfield with V-twin-cylinder Moto-sacoche engine, dating from 1908 and photographed at Middlesbrough 64 years later. Note chain drive and spoon-type rear brake.

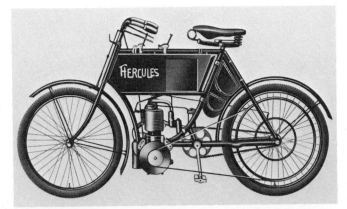

10B Hercules

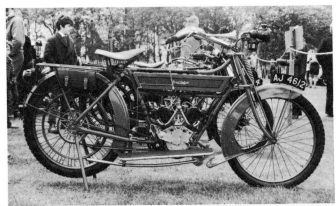

10E Royal Enfield

11A: One of the most successful and longest lasting British marques was the Triumph. This 1911 single-geared model, fitted with a hub clutch, had a single-cylinder $3\frac{1}{2}$ HP side-valve engine with direct-belt drive from engine pulley to rear wheel, the most common design configuration at the time. Note the magneto, protected by a shield, in front of the engine.

11B: Belgian FN with shaft drive of 1912. The single-cylinder side-valve engine of 285 cc (65 × 86 mm) was placed transversally and had magneto ignition. Tyre size was 26 × $2\frac{3}{8}$.

11A Triumph

11C: NUT motorcycle with V-twin JAP engine, photographed with its proud owner, a Mr P. J. Evans, in 1912. NUT stood for Newcastle-upon-Tyne, the place near which the manufacturers, The NUT Engine and Cycle Co., had their works. The 'strapped-on' fuel tank was a distinguishable feature of the marque.

11D: In 1912 a Scott motorcycle was experimentally fitted with a Laird-Menteyne machine gun by Coventry Ordnance (Cammell Laird & Co.). A special front stand allowed full-lock traverse of the gun, which swung with the handlebars. The Scott had a parallel twin-cyl. two-stroke engine.

11B FN

11D Scott

# THE EARLY YEARS

12: It was not long after the motorcycle had become a commercial proposition and achieved a reasonable standard of efficiency and reliability that it was used for various types of sporting events such as trials, road and track races, hill-climbs, etc. The unidentified gentleman with his heavy 1903/04 Excelsior looks rightly pleased with his magnificent display of trophies and other prizes. The Excelsior was one of several machines using a Belgian Minerva engine (originally designed in 1899 by two Swiss engineers).

13A (above): Members of an early motorcycle club with their machines (Excelsiors, Rex and Singers). The picture was taken prior to 1904, this being the year when number plates became compulsory.
13B: A duel in the 100-mile race at the Brooklands race track in 1910, with a V-twin being just ahead of a 'one-lunger'.
13C: Pitstop . . . and feverish activity. Crash helmets were, amazingly, not worn in those days, when maximum speeds were in the order of 60 mph. Note the completely smooth tyre.

13B Brooklands, 1910

13C Pitstop . . .

# THE EARLY YEARS

14A Triumph

14B Triumph/Merryweather

14C Humber

14A: From about 1903 the sidecar became the most popular mode of carrying passengers. It replaced the earlier uncomfortable and unsafe two-wheeled armchair trailers which used to be towed behind motor-bicycles (see page 7). The motortricycle was also to be ousted by the sidecar combination. Illustrated is an early 'Triumph with chair', photographed in Singapore. Note the wickerwork sidecar 'body', complete with door. Later came enclosed models with accommodation for several passengers.

14B: Sidecar combinations were used even as the basis for light fire appliances, exemplified by this British Merryweather unit delivered to Parana, Argentina, in 1913. The equipment included a small pump, driven from the machine's V-twin engine. A later model is shown on page 38.

14C: This magnificent and impressive early Humber sidecar combination was probably a prototype. It had a water-cooled engine. Humber motorcycle production ceased during the Great Depression of the early 'thirties.

15A Autocarrier

15A : AC Cars Ltd of Thames Ditton, Surrey, started their business producing three-wheelers, including the Auto-carrier (hence the initials). In 1910 the company, then based in West Norwood, London, and known as Autocars and Accessories Ltd, supplied four Autocarriers to the 25th County of London Cyclist Regiment. Two were equipped with Maxim machine guns (shown) ; the other two carried spare ammunition. They had an air-cooled single-cylinder four-stroke engine of 5·6 HP (90 × 102 mm) with two flywheels. Further details were as follows : transmission : flexible chain sprocket on engine shaft, Reynolds chain drive to special two-speed grease-packed gear set on rear wheel ; clutch : multiple-disc type, working in oil, with hand lever on the tiller-type steering column ; petrol tank : 2¼ gallons, sufficient for 75 to 100 miles ; brakes : two, 'especially powerful in backward direc-tion . . . .' ; frame : ash members reinforced by strong side panels of birch wood ; carrying capacity : 4–5 cwt.

15B Eysink

15B : The Dutch firm of Eysink in Amersfoort in 1906/07 offered a wide range of motor-cycles of various types, including this 2¾-HP Tri-car with wickerwork passenger seat. A seat of aluminium sheet on ash framework was also available, as was goods carrying bodywork.

15C : The British Army had been using motorcycles since the early 1900s and the first purpose-built machines were supplied by Messrs A. W. Wall Ltd of Guildford in 1906. The picture shows military 'push'- and motor-bikes during manoeuvres shortly before the First World War (*see* following section). The machine in the centre is a BSA.

15C BSA

## THE FIRST WORLD WAR

16A Douglas

16A: The most widely used marques of motorcycles employed by the British armed forces in the 1914–18 war were the Douglas (shown) and the Triumph (q.v.). Of the Douglas the Army used many thousands of 2¾-HP solo machines and 4-HP sidecar-combinations.

16B Douglas

16B: Douglas 2¾-HP solo machine, fully equipped for military use.

16C: Dynamometer, 1917-style. A Douglas engine on the test bench in a British Army workshop in France. The Douglas flat-twin was first conceived in 1905 by Joseph Barter and was in production for many years.

16C Douglas

17A Triumph

17B: The Triumph Cycle Co. were the largest British suppliers of military motorcycles and this, the $3\frac{1}{2}$-HP WD model, was the most numerous. It had a single-cylinder four-stroke power unit with bore and stroke of 85 × 88 mm, driving through a Sturmey-Archer three-speed gearbox with kick-starter. Because of its reliability the Triumph became popularly known as the 'Trusty'.

17C: One of the many roles of motor-cyclists in the First World War was that of pigeon carrier. This picture shows a pair of Triumphs used for this purpose.

17D: Typical picture postcard as sent to the folks at home by British 'Tommies' in France.

17C Triumph

17A: Production of motorcycles for civilian use in Britain gradually decreased after 1914 and came to a halt in late 1916, following which date production was exclusively for the British Government and their Allies. This civilian 'Baby' Triumph of 1916 has survived to this day and was probably one of the last non-military machines of that period. It has a single-cylinder 225-cc two-stroke push-start engine of $2\frac{1}{4}$ HP and features the typical Triumph front forks with (nearly) horizontally-placed coil spring. It was re-introduced after the war and built until 1923, designated Junior Light Weight Type LW. Standing alongside is a 1924 BSA.

17B Triumph

17D 'Somewhere in France'

# THE FIRST WORLD WAR

18A/B/C: Although the Netherlands remained neutral during the 1914–18 war, the Dutch Army was comparatively well-equipped with motor vehicles, albeit mainly impressed civilian types. Numbers of Eysink motorcycles, however, were purpose-built for carrying machine guns, which could be turned back-to-front for maximum elevation. Fig. 18A shows the basic machine, which featured special front forks with heavy-duty suspension and support legs, as well as ammunition cases on either side.
Eysink had been producing motorcycles of various types since 1901 and manufactured practically all the components, including the engines, in their own factory. The major bought-out items were the carburettor (AMAC), the magneto (Bosch) and the tyres. The engine of the machine shown was a 3½-HP single-cylinder side-valve unit with bore and stroke of 74 × 95 mm and kick-starter (optional extra on civilian models). Figs. 18B and 18C show the machines in action during manoeuvres.

18B Eysink

18A Eysink

18C Eysink

19A: One of the motorcycles used in large numbers by the US Army was the Indian M1917, produced by the Hendee Mfg.Co. of Springfield, Massachusetts. It had a 61-cu.in V-twin-cylinder engine with Wheeler & Schebler carburettor, Dixie magneto ignition and three-speed gearbox. The unusual sprung wheels shown in this photograph were, in fact, an experimental modification in 1920.

19A Indian

19B Bianchi

19B: The Italian forces, too, used many motorcycles. Illustrated is one of their most numerous models of the First World War: the *Motociclo Bianchi tipo A* of 1914.

19C: Another popular Italian marque at the time was the Frera, in solo and sidecar form. The subject of this 1917 advertisement was the firm's 8/10-HP 1140-cc V-twin machine. 4-HP single-cylinder models were also made. The Germans, too, employed many motorcycles. (For additional coverage *see: The Observer's Army Vehicles Directory—to 1940.*)

19C Frera

# THE FIRST WORLD WAR

20 Harley-Davidson

20: Harley-Davidson, Hendee/Indian (*q.v.*) and Cleveland were the three major suppliers of American military motorcycles, solo as well as sidecar combinations. The picture shows a demonstration of a Harley-Davidson combination with machine gun and armour shield.

21B  Clyno/Vickers

21B: The Clyno Engineering Co. of Wolverhampton, in conjunction with Vickers Ltd, developed a motorcycle combination for use by the Motor Machine Gun Corps in 1915. It was used mainly as a mobile mount for the Maxim-type machine gun. The machine had a 5–6-HP wide-angle V-twin engine with 76 × 82 mm bore and stroke, three-speed gearbox and chain drive. Machine gun carriers were also supplied by several other motorcycle manufacturers.

21C: Sidecars were widely used in the 1914–18 war, for a variety of purposes. Note the full weather protection for the passenger of this medical unit. The front end of the sidecar body consisted of a large locker with forward-hinged lid. A spare wheel was carried at the rear.

21D  Scott

21A  Indian

21A: Indian sidecar ambulance, used during the First World War by the British Red Cross Society. Note that these American machines, like most American cars and trucks, had left-hand drive, i.e. the sidecar was attached to the right-hand side. This also applied to other countries where the rule of the road is, or was, to drive on the right.

21C  Royal Enfield

21D: Scott Motor Cycle Co. of Yorkshire were the producers of the legendary twin-cylinder two-stroke machines of this name. The water-cooled cylinders were placed side by side and inclined forward. With periodical improvements this design was in production for more than 20 years and the marque had many ardent followers.

# THE FIRST WORLD WAR

22  British WD motorcycles awaiting overhaul in France, 1917

22 : The British armed forces in France during the 1914–18 war utilized tens of thousands of motorcycles, in addition to numerous four-wheeled vehicles. By 1916/17 the Army had set up large MT (Motor Transport) Base Heavy-Repair Workshops at St Omer in Northern France for repairing and reconditioning war-worn and/or -damaged vehicles. These pages illustrate various departments of the motorcycle section. Fig. 22 shows the 'Casualty Department' where machines of all kinds were taken in for rebuilding. Douglas solo machines and sidecar combinations dominate this scene. The pictures were taken in the summer of 1917.

23B

23A

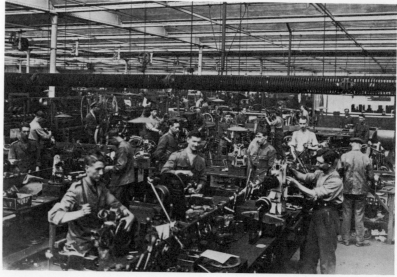

23A : From the outside casualty park the machines were taken inside for complete dismantling. Nearest the camera are some Triumph 'Trusty' solos.

23B : The brazing department, where frames (including those of sidecars) and forks were straightened and repaired.

23C : In the engine repair shop the power units were completely rebuilt. After testing, these engines were transferred to the erection shops, shown on the following pages.

23C

# THE FIRST WORLD WAR

24A

24A: A batch of rebuilt Triumph 'Trusty' and Douglas flat-twin engines and gearboxes in the test shop. The British Army had standardized on these two makes and most of the overhaul work was concentrated on these machines. Other makes, including vast quantities of pre-war impressed civilian types, were often rejected after they had finished their useful life or been damaged in combat or road accidents. The RAF used chiefly the Phelon & Moore (Panther) single-cylinder 3½-HP solo machine but by far the majority of these were used at home, i.e. in the UK. For more details of makes and quantities see page 26.

24C

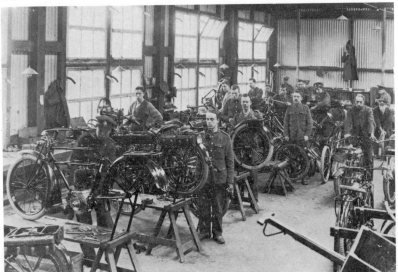

24B

24B/C: Two views in the erection shop, showing Triumph and Douglas machines respectively. This is where the final assembly took place from rebuilt and new components. Compared with their colleagues in the trenches, these soldiers had a relatively easy life and not a few of them continued in the motorcycle business after demob!

25: Final inspection and preparing the as-new machines for re-issue to the Army in the field.

25 Douglas and Triumph WD machines being made ready for re-issue.

# THE FIRST WORLD WAR

Makes and quantities of motorcycles and sidecars in possession of the British Armed Forces at the time of the armistice in 1918*

| Make | Overseas** | At Home | Total in Service | Remarks |
|---|---|---|---|---|
| AJS | 262 | 8 | 270 | 250 in Italy |
| Ariel | 27 | 25 | 52 | |
| Autocarrier | — | 12 | 12 | three-wheelers |
| Bradbury | 1 | 14 | 15 | |
| BSA | 322 | 766 | 1,088 | 245 in E. Africa |
| Clyno | 642 | 1,150 | 1,792 | 478 in France |
| Douglas | 9,515 | 8,800 | 18,315 | incl. 13,477 2¾-HP solo and 4,816 4-HP combinations |
| Humber | 2 | 9 | 11 | |
| Indian | 33 | 140 | 173 | 105 with Canadian Contingent |
| James | 155 | 8 | 163 | 155 in Italy |
| Matchless | 1 | 135 | 136 | also 8 Matchless sidecars |
| New Hudson | 7 | 14 | 21 | |
| New Imperial | 88 | 338 | 426 | 646 Sunbeam side-cars for same |
| Norton | — | 232 | 232 | |
| Phelon & Moore | 135 | 3,248 | 3,383 | Standardized by RAF; also 150 P & M sidecars |
| Premier | 6 | 50 | 56 | |
| Rover | 20 | 366 | 386 | also 210 Rover sidecars |
| Royal Ruby | 51 | 104 | 155 | 163 Mills-Fulford sidecars for same |
| Royal Enfield | 1 | 160 | 161 | |
| Rudge Multi | 18 | 377 | 395 | also 4 Rudge sidecars |
| Scott | — | 411 | 411 | also 1 Scott sidecar |
| Sunbeam | 1 | 78 | 79 | also 326 Sunbeam sidecars |
| Triumph | 9,813 | 8,185 | 17,998 | mainly 4 HP; 306 sidecars for same*** |
| Warwick | — | 15 | 15 | |
| Zenith | 5 | 304 | 309 | |

26 After the war thousands of vehicles were auctioned at Government Motor Sales.

* Only those makes are listed of which more than ten units were in service; other makes, with total quantities in parentheses, were: Abingdon (1), BAT (2), Brennabor (2), Burney & Blackburne (1), Calthorpe (1), Campion (4), Centaur (1), FN (1), Griffon (1), Harley-Davidson (1), Imperial (1), JAP (2), Lea-Francis (9), Levis (1), LMC (1), Magnet (1), Motosacoche (1), NUT (7), NSU (2), OK Junior (1), Quadrant (6), Regal (1), Rex (1), Singer (6), Sparkbrook (1), Sun (1), Wanderer (1).
Listed as 'sidecars only' were 243 Empires. The grand total of these official records amounted to 48,175 units. Number of war losses and other rejects is not known.

** Overseas territories and quantities were: East Africa (563), Egypt (1461), France (15,978), India (289), Italy (1022), Malta (17), Mesopotamia (1314), Russia (40), Salonica (976). Grand total overseas: 21,660.

*** Sidecars: Gloria (103), Holbrook (18), Triumph (167), Willowbrook (18).

27A Adria

27B AJS

The 7 h.p. A.J.S. Passenger Combination.

7 h.p. Twin Cylinder Engine, 74×93 m/m Bore and Stroke, 800 c.c., All-Chain Drive, Three-speed Gear, Hand-controlled Clutch, Kick-starter, Quick Detachable Interchangeable Wheels, 700×80 m/m Dunlop Tyres, Brampton "Biflex" Spring Forks, Internal Expanding Front and Rear Brakes, Lucas "Magdyno" Electric Lighting Set, Lucas Bulb Horn, Brooks Cantilever Saddle, Amac Carburetter, Hans Renold Chains. Windscreen, Celluloid Sidescreen, Stormproof Apron and Tools.

Price to standard specification, less Spare
Wheel and Tyre and Hood .. **£152 : 10**

## Proved Merit.

THE luxury and refinement of modern Motor Cycling are truly exemplified in A.J.S. Motor Cycles. The equipment and specification include nothing but the very best, whilst on a value for money basis alone they have no equal. A.J.S. Motor Cycles are the logical outcome of over 15 years specialised concentration in the designing and manufacture of Motor Cycles.

The name A.J.S. is a guarantee of all that is best in British Motor Cycling Engineering practice. Their sterling qualities have been abundantly proved by the consistent reliability and service in the hands of private owners, whilst their record of success in trials and competitions all over the world, extending over many years, has also won for them a unique and unrivalled position.

The 2¾ h.p. A.J.S. Standard Touring Model.

All-chain Drive, Three-speed Gear, Hand-controlled Clutch, Kick-starter, Quick Detachable Rear Wheel, Internal Expanding Front and Rear Brakes, Brooks B150 Saddle, 650×65 m/m Hutchinson Heavy Rubber Studded Tyres .. **£69**

The 2¾ h.p. A.J.S. Standard Sporting Model.

All-chain Drive, Three-speed Gear, Hand-controlled Clutch, Kick-starter, Quick Detachable Rear Wheel, Internal Expanding Front and Rear Brakes, Brooks B150 Saddle, 650×65 m/m Hutchinson Heavy Rubber Studded Tyres .. **£69**

The 2¾ h.p. A.J.S. Overhead Valve T.T. Model.

All-chain Drive, Three-speed Gear, Hand-controlled Clutch, Quick Detachable Rear Wheel, Internal Expanding Front and Rear Brakes, Brooks B150 Saddle, 650 × 65 m/m Hutchinson Heavy Rubber Studded Tyres .. **£75**

Write for the
**A.J.S. CATALOGUE**
illustrating
and
describing
our Full Range
of Motor cycles.

*Sent Post Free on request.*

## A·J·S Motor Cycles

A. J. STEVENS & CO. (1914), LTD.,
WOLVERHAMPTON.

*London Agents:*
H. Taylor & Co., Ltd., 52-53, Sussex Place,
South Kensington, S.W.7.

Recent A.J.S.
Successes include:—

THE FRENCH GRAND
PRIX RACE,
THE SCOTTISH SPEED
CHAMPIONSHIP,
and
THE IRISH FIFTY-FIVE
MILES ROAD RACE.

All won by the
2¾ h.p. A.J.S.

27A: After the First World War countless new makes of motorcycles appeared, but few of the new manufacturers stayed in business for long. The Adria was one, made for only a few years, until 1923, in Saxony, Germany. Two models were offered, both four-strokes of conventional design.

27B: AJS 350-cc with big-port overhead-valve engine of 1927, stripped down for road racing.

27C: AJS (A. J. Stevens) had commenced motorcycle production in 1909, after having made engines, frames and other components for other manufacturers. This advertisement shows the company's offerings in the autumn of 1923. By this time most motorcycles had proper gearboxes, behind the engine, with kick-starter and chain drive (rather than the outdated direct belt drive, chain-and-pedal starting and rear hub gears), lower saddle position (usually by curving the frame top tube), front brakes (instead of rear only), much-improved tyres, etc. Electric lighting sets, with a dynamo, also became more common.

# THE TWENTIES

28A AJS

28B Ariel

28C: BD (Breitfeld & Danek) was a Czech manufacturer and the machine illustrated is a 500-cc OHV model as delivered in 1926 to the Czech Army, where it was used both solo and with sidecar. It had Bosch magneto ignition, three-speed gearbox, 26 × 3 tyres and weighed 150 kg.

28D: One of the most impressive of British machines was the Brough. George Brough, at one time the fastest man on two wheels, had decided in 1919 to build motorcycles of his own design and until 1940 produced the expensive but superb Brough Superior, or the 'Rolls-Royce of motorcycles'. Shown is the 996-cc JAP V-twin-engined 1926 model of the equally legendary 'Lawrence of Arabia', who from 1922 successively owned eight machines of this marque—'the jolliest things on wheels' he called them in a letter to George Brough.

28C BD

28A: AJS R7 racing machine was developed in 1929/30 from the firm's 1927 works racers. They had overhead-cam engines with enclosed chain drive. The R7 remained in production during the 1930s, with various modifications and improvements.

28B: Ariel, another big name in the British motorcycle industry, and another firm which had made 'push-bikes' before producing motorcycles (from 1903). Shown is a 1928 500-cc OHV road machine, modified for short circuit racing.

28D Brough

29A: BSA Cycles Ltd was an outgrowth of the British Small Arms Co., which had taken up motorcycle manufacture in 1910 (following experiments going back to 1905 and production of bicycles from about 1880). This advertisement lists the BSA models which were available in late 1925.

29B: While most of the world's motorcycles were rather similar in general design, various unusual, sometimes revolutionary, machines saw the light of day. This peculiar model, a Cechie-Böhmerland, was made in Czechoslovakia in 1927 by Albin Liebisch. It had a 16-HP 600-cc OHV engine, driving through a three-speed gearbox. The wheels were made of aluminium alloy and the machine weighed about 170 kg. Maximum speed was claimed to be 95 km/h. Two fuel tanks were placed at the rear, on either side of the wheel.

29B Cechie-Böhmerland

# POPULARITY YOUR GUIDE

**B.S.A.**
**2·49** h.p. de Luxe

with **3-speed**, clutch, kick-starter, mechanical and grease gun lubrication, Terry spring seat saddle, shock absorbers, and all-chain drive.

**£37 . 10s.**

| B.S.A. | | | B.S.A. | | |
|---|---|---|---|---|---|
| 2·49 h.p., 2-speed, all-chain drive | · | £36. 0s. | 5·57 h.p., 3-speed | - - - - - | £55 |
| 2·49 h.p. De Luxe, 3-speed | - - - | £37.10s. | 5·57 h.p. De Luxe, 3-speed | - - - - | £60 |
| 3·49 h.p., 3-speed | - - - - - | £41.15s. | 7·70 h.p., Twin Cylinder, 3-speed | - - | £63 |
| 3·49 h.p. O.H.V. De Luxe, 3-speed | - | £47. 0s. | 7·70 h.p. De Luxe, Twin Cylinder | - | £69 |
| 4·93 h.p., 3-speed | - - - - - | £44.15s. | 9·86 h.p., Twin Cylinder, 3-speed | - - | £64 |
| 4·93 h.p. De Luxe, 3-speed | - - - | £48.15s. | 9·86 h.p. De Luxe, Twin Cylinder | - | £70 |
| | | | 9·86 h.p. Colonial, Twin Cylinder | - | £70 |

**B.S.A.**
**3·49** h.p. Comb.

3-speed, clutch, kickstarter, mechanical and grease gun lubrication, all-chain drive, with No. 9c Sidecar.

**£52 . 15s.**

29A BSA

There is definite proof on every road of the popularity of B.S.A. Motor Bicycles. This popularity is your safest guide when buying a new machine. And remember, every B.S.A. is backed by the most efficient motor cycle Spares and Repair Service in the world.

In the leading article of the "Daily Mail" on October 13th, 1925, British Motor Cycles received the following tribute: "It is admitted by all authorities that the British Motor Cycle is not only the best in the world but also much the best." In the British Motor Cycle industry one name stands pre-eminent—

# B·S·A

## the undisputed leader

**Write for Catalogue and Terms**

B.S.A. Cycles Ltd., 47, Small Heath, Birmingham.    Prop's: The Birmingham Small Arms Co., Ltd.

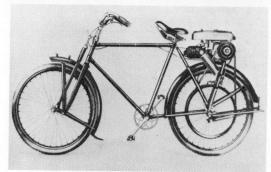

29C DKW

29C: In 1920/21 the Dane, Jörgen Skafte Rasmussen, who lived in Saxony, Germany, introduced a small two-stroke engine (designed by Hugo Ruppe) which clipped onto a conventional bicycle, driving the rear wheel by means of a leather belt. So successful was this 122-cc auxiliary engine that by August 1922 some 25,000 units had been sold. It was called DKW, derived from *Das Kleine Wunder* (the little miracle).

# THE TWENTIES

30A DKW

30B DKW

30C Douglas, etc.

30A: During 1921–22 DKW (i.e. the Zchopauer Motorenwerke J. S. Rasmussen in Zchopau, Saxony, Germany) produced some 'mobile armchairs', of which this was the first. Named the Golem-Roller, it had a horizontal 122-cc two-stroke engine (like the auxiliary engine shown in Fig. 29C). In 1922 it was superseded by an improved 142-cc model, known as the Lomos-Roller. Relatively few were made.

30B: DKW produced various types of motorcycles, all with two-stroke engines (many of which were also supplied to other manufacturers). This Model SM (steel model) featured an advanced pressed-steel frame—a design which was later adopted also by several other motorcycle makers. The SM had a 173-cc engine and first appeared in 1924.

30C: A happy-looking group of military motorcyclists in Singapore in the late 1920s. The machine in the centre is a 1928 Douglas 4½-HP with 600-cc flat-twin engine; immediately behind it is a Raleigh. On the left poses a Sunbeam Lion OHV model of 1927 and on the far right is a New Hudson.

31B FN

31C FN

31D FN

31A: The Swedish Monark company commenced motorcycle production in 1920, initially under the name Esse. It was a pedal-assist chain-drive machine with a 172-cc single-cylinder power unit.

31A Esse

31B: FN in Belgium, the famous Fabrique Nationale des Armes de Guerre at Herstal, near Liège, had been producing single- and four-cylinder motorcycles for many years and in 1922 launched this 346-cc Model M60 with exposed overhead valves and a bore and stroke of 70·5 × 80·5 mm. The machine weighed a modest 125 kg and could achieve 85 km/h. Note the spoon-type brakes on 'dummy rims', front and rear, the acetylene lighting set, the 'U'-shaped leaf spring in the front forks and the open exhaust.

31C: FN's 350-cc side-valve M70 was a very reliable machine, produced from 1927/28 until the mid-thirties. Shown is the 'Sahara' version of 1928. The flywheel was exposed, on the right-hand side, earning it the nickname of 'the grindstone'.

31D: From 1905 until well into the twenties FN produced their famous four-cylinder machines. The specimen illustrated dates from 1919/20. It had an air-cooled 748-cc (52 × 88 mm) in-line engine with three-speed gearbox, foot-controlled multi-plate clutch, kick-starter and shaft drive. In Britain it sold at £160.

## THE TWENTIES

32A Henderson

32A: Henderson was an American producer of heavy four-in-line engined machines. This combination, with sidecar on the left-hand side dates from 1929 and has survived in Great Britain where it is owned by Mr Fred Fricker, a member of the American Motorcycle Register. It has a three-speed gearbox, with hand lever on the left, and chain drive. Note the large finned drum brakes.

32B: The Indian Motorcycle Co. (formerly the Hendee Mfg.Co.) of Springfield, Mass., USA, produced large numbers of side-valve V-twins for many years. Shown is a 598-cc (70 × 78 mm) Scout, as made during the mid-twenties. The clutch was operated by a pedal on the left; the gearbox had three speeds. Maximum speed was about 110 km/h.

32B Indian

32C Indian

32C: Indians, like Harley-Davidsons, were widely used in police and military roles. Shown is a sidecar combination of the Argentine Army, photographed in November 1925.

32D Moto Guzzi

32D: The first series-production Italian Moto Guzzi was this Standard 500 model of 1921–24. Some of the basic features of its engine were found in Moto Guzzis for many years to come: horizontal cylinder with detachable head and opposed valves (side inlet, overhead exhaust), external flywheel, anti-clockwise crankshaft rotation, hairpin valve springs, etc. The Standard 500 (499 cc, 88 × 82 mm) developed 13·2 HP and had a three-speed gearbox, built-in unit with the engine. Top speed was 100 km/h.

33A: The first Monark motorcycle left the factory in Varberg, Sweden, in 1925. Earlier machines produced by this firm were called Esse (*see* 31A).

33B: Sheffield-Simplex of Kingston-on-Thames during the early 1920s offered the peculiar Ner-a-Car, designed by the American C. A. Neracher, and sometimes unkindly referred to as the 'motor-assisted mudguard'. It bristled with unconventional features, such as variable friction-drive transmission and hub-centre steering. This advertisement appeared in September 1923.

33A  Monark

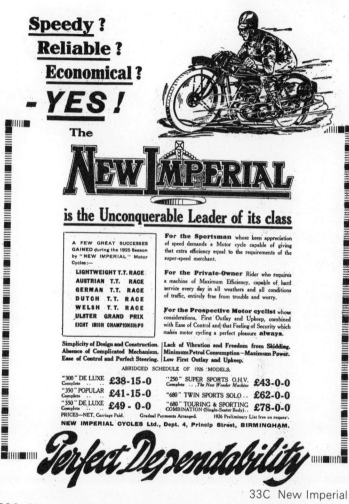

Speedy?
Reliable?
Economical?
- YES!

The

# NEW IMPERIAL

## is the Unconquerable Leader of its class

A FEW GREAT SUCCESSES GAINED during the 1925 Season by "NEW IMPERIAL" Motor Cycles:—

LIGHTWEIGHT T.T. RACE
AUSTRIAN T.T. RACE
GERMAN T.T. RACE
DUTCH T.T. RACE
WELSH T.T. RACE
ULSTER GRAND PRIX
EIGHT IRISH CHAMPIONSHIPS

For the Sportsman whose keen appreciation of speed demands a Motor cycle capable of giving that extra efficiency equal to the requirements of the super-speed merchant.

For the Private-Owner Rider who requires a machine of Maximum Efficiency, capable of hard service every day in all weathers and all conditions of traffic, entirely free from trouble and worry.

For the Prospective Motor cyclist whose considerations, First Outlay and Upkeep, combined with Ease of Control and that Feeling of Security which makes motor cycling a perfect pleasure always.

Simplicity of Design and Construction. Absence of Complicated Mechanism. Ease of Control and Perfect Steering.

Lack of Vibration and Freedom from Skidding. Minimum Petrol Consumption—Maximum Power. Low First Outlay and Upkeep.

ABRIDGED SCHEDULE OF 1926 MODELS.

| | | | |
|---|---|---|---|
| "300" DE LUXE Complete | £38-15-0 | "250" SUPER SPORTS O.H.V. Complete .. ..The New Wonder Machine | £43-0-0 |
| "350" POPULAR Complete | £41-15-0 | "680" TWIN SPORTS SOLO .. | £62-0-0 |
| "350" DE LUXE Complete | £49-0-0 | "680" TOURING & SPORTING COMBINATION (Single-Seater Body).. | £78-0-0 |

PRICES—NET, Carriage Paid.    Gradual Payments Arranged.    1926 Preliminary List free on request.

NEW IMPERIAL CYCLES Ltd., Dept. 4, Princip Street, BIRMINGHAM.

*Perfect Dependability*

33C  New Imperial

33C: New Imperial was a well-known make between the wars. This late-1925 advertisement lists part of the Birmingham firm's production programme for the 1926 model year. Other British makes of the early and mid-twenties which used the prefix 'New' included New Comet, New Coulson, New Era, New Gerrard, New Hudson, New Knight, New Paragon, and New Scale.

## Some outstanding features of the

B Model

# NER-A-CAR

## No. 1 The Transmission:

Disc Drive and Final Chain.

FLY-WHEEL
KICK STARTER
CHAIN TO REAR WHEEL
DRIVEN DISC
TRANS-MISSION SHAFT
FRAME MEMBERS

each speed is equally silent and efficient. Disc carried on transmission shaft parallel to flywheel and running on self-aligning ball bearings. Only one chain, to rear wheel, and it is quickly adjustable for stretch. Twist grip clutch control from handle bar.

Thanks to the low riding position, correct weight distribution, car type steering and stability, efficient brakes, simplicity of control, and scientifically designed mudguards and undershield, the "B" Model Ner-a-Car is the **SAFEST and CLEANEST Motor Cycle made**. It will maintain a good average speed all day and climb any hill with ease.

The only successful friction-driven motor cycle in existence. The principle results in great simplicity, ease of control and smooth running. Five distinct speeds are provided so that the engine can be kept at its most efficient and economical speed always. There are no gears to crash and

Price £65, fully equipped, with electric light, carriage paid.

*Write for Catalogue from the Manufacturers:*

**The Sheffield-Simplex Company,**

Ner-a-Car Works, Canbury Park Road, Kingston-on-Thames.

33B  Ner-a-Car

# THE TWENTIES

The **Unapproachable** *Norton*
REGD. TRADE MARK

## Sets Another Standard

TWO NORTON Motorcycles assembled from stock parts under A.C.U. OBSERVATION, one solo and one sidecar, completed 3,190½ miles in 14 riding days over the most severe roads in England and Scotland. The same machines still under A.C.U. observation captured 32 WORLD'S RECORDS for long distances at Brooklands, including the twelve hours for each class, thus proving once again that the NORTON Standard is unapproachable, and that anyone can buy a NORTON of equal excellence.

| 1926 | Prices | | |
|---|---|---|---|
| Model No. 16H, 4.90 h.p. | £59 | 10 | 0 |
| Model No 2, 4.90 h.p. | £62 | 0 | 0 |
| Model No. 17C, 4.90 h.p. | £63 | 0 | 0 |
| No. 1, "Big Four" 6.33 h.p. | £65 | 0 | 0 |
| No. 14, "Big Four" 6.33 h.p. | £70 | 0 | 0 |
| No. 18, 4.90 h.p. O.H.V. | £72 | 0 | 0 |
| No. 19, 5.88 h.p. O.H.V. | £77 | 0 | 0 |
| No. 24, 5.88 h.p. O.H.V. | £82 | 0 | 0 |

*Catalogue on request.*

Norton Motors Ltd
**Bracebridge Street BIRMINGHAM**

34A Norton

34A : Norton, a name almost synonymous with British motorcycles, commenced production in 1898 and later became the greatest name in the history of motorcycle racing, winning no fewer than 34 TTs (Tourist Trophy races), hundreds of major Grand Prix races and countless other events, all over the world. By far the majority of these legendary machines were big 'singles'. This advertisement appeared in late 1925.

34B : The NUT V-twin for 1924 still featured the characteristic drilled strips around the fuel tank. The 5-HP engine, with magneto ignition and a semi-automatic lubrication system, drove through a three-speed Sturmey-Archer countershaft gearbox. It weighed 252 pounds and the price was later reduced to £68.

34B NUT

34C NV

34C : In 1926 the first Swedish NV motorcycle appeared. It was made entirely in Sweden, the engine, a single OHV unit, by Nymans of Uppsala.

34D : The OEC was a product of Osborn Engineering Co. Ltd, of Gosport, Hampshire. Illustrated is a 500-cc JAP-engined short-circuit racer of 1928/29.

34D OEC

# THE TWENTIES

35A Praga

35A: Praga motorcycles were made by Praga-CKD in Prague, Czechoslovakia, and this 500-cc Model BD—the 'Bedar'—was quite numerous. Introduced in 1928 it remained in production until 1934. The 15-HP single-cylinder (84 × 90 mm) engine had twin overhead camshafts and drove through a three-speed gearbox. Maximum speed, solo, was 105 km/h, with sidecar 80 km/h. The BD was originally made by Breitfeld & Danek, hence the initials (see 28C).

35B: Puch, of Austria, offered at least eight different models during the 1920s, including this Model LM, a 122·2-cc (2 × 36 × 60 mm) dual-piston two-stroke in 1923. It developed 2 HP and, weighing only 42 kg, was good for 60 km/h.

35C: The Puch LM II 'Monza' racer of 1924 also had dual pistons but was a transverse vertical twin of 350-cc cubic capacity. Each pair of pistons had a Y-shaped connecting rod. Cylinder bore and piston stroke were 40 and 70 mm respectively and the engine developed 5 HP at 2500 rpm. Shown is an 'exploded view' of the engine (see Fig. 36A for the complete machine).

35B Puch

35C Puch

# THE TWENTIES

**36A**: Puch LM II 'Monza' racing motorcycle of 1924 had a 350-cc twin engine (*see* Fig. 35D) with two speeds and a further two speeds in the rear hub. The machine weighed 100 kg and had a maximum speed of about 85 km/h. Tyre size was 26 × 3.

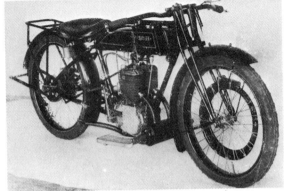

36A Puch

**36B**: Royal Enfield Model LW (Lightweight) of the early 1920s had a 2¼-HP (64 × 70 mm) two-stroke engine and the makers' own two-speed gearbox. The price was £65 in 1921, £55 in 1922, £50 in 1923 and dropped to £42 in 1924.

## An Ideal Lightweight Model.

The 2¼ h.p. Royal Enfield Two-stroke motor cycle is ideal for "solo work." It is very light yet exceptionally strong and embodies the Enfield Patent Two-speed and Free-engine gear, and Cush Drive Hub.

Simplicity of control is manifest in the highest degree—one lever only controlling the speed of the machine. Fixed ignition is used and in conjunction with the A.M.A.C. single lever automatic carburettor the riding attention is reduced to an absolute minimum.

*Further particulars gladly sent on request.*

**The ENFIELD CYCLE CO., LTD., REDDITCH.**

36B Royal Enfield

**36C**: Rudge-Whitworth had been producing many types of motorcycles, including (from 1911/12) the famous Rudge 'Multis' which had a belt-drive variable-ratio transmission system with movable pulley flanges on the engine shaft and the rear wheel. In the mid-1920s a new range of machines appeared, featuring four-valve engines, four-speed gearboxes and coupled brakes. Shown is the firm's 4·99-HP (15-bhp) Touring Combination for 1926.

## The 1926 Motor Bicycle Combination

The Rudge-Whitworth 4·99 H.P. Motor Bicycle, that already has proved so popular, must obviously be equally efficient with a sidecar. Here are the Rudge-Whitworth 1926 Sidecars. There is a Touring model for the regular Motor Cyclist, and a very attractive Streamline Sporting Sidecar for the Speedman. The Chassis, in all cases, has a flat laminated spring steel axle, and cross members are built into triangular shape. The body rides on a transverse laminated spring at rear and a curved flat spring at front. Four point attachment is a feature of all Rudge-Whitworth Combinations, and a Rudge-Whitworth Detachable Wheel, interchangeable with those of the Motor Bicycle, is fitted to all sidecars. Write for full particulars of Rudge-Whitworth Sidecars and

### "The Motor Bicycle of 1926."

| | |
|---|---|
| The Rudge-Whitworth four valve, four-speed, 4·99 H.P. 15 B.H.P. Motor Bicycle | £46.0.0 |
| The Rudge-Whitworth Touring Sidecar *with Locker Space for 2 suit cases, etc.* | £18.0.0 |
| The Rudge-Whitworth Streamline Sporting Sidecar | £20.0.0 |

## Rudge-Whitworth, Ltd., Coventry.

London : 230, Tottenham Court Road, W.1.     Manchester : 192, Deansgate.
Birmingham : 145, Corporation Street.     Bristol : 61, Queen's Road

By Appointment
Cycle Makers to
H.M. King George

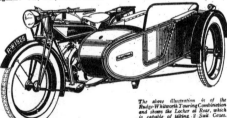

*The above illustration is of the Rudge-Whitworth Touring Combination and shows the Locker at Rear, which is capable of taking 2 Suit Cases.*

**Rudge-Whitworth** FOUR VALVE FOUR SPEED

36C Rudge-Whitworth

37A Scott

feature of the combination shown was the interchangeability of all three wheels. Prices for 1924 were considerably lower than those of 1923. The manufacturers' address is noteworthy.

37C: In the immediate post-WWI years there was a brief boom in motor scooters and ultra-lightweight cyclecars. The Unibus, looking many years ahead of its time, was produced by the Gloucestershire Aircraft Co. of Cheltenham but by 1923 had disappeared.

37A: The Scott Motor Cycle Co in Shipley, Yorkshire, continued their superb two-stroke machines which were of unconventional and immediately recognizable design. The unusual transverse twin-cylinder engines had thermo-syphon water-cooling and from 1924 they had an engine-operated oiling system, replacing the earlier semi-automatic configuration. This advertisement dates from 1925.

37B: The 1923 Sunbeam $4\frac{1}{4}$-HP had a single-cylinder 85 × 105-mm side-valve engine with three-speed gearbox and totally-enclosed chain drive. A

37B Sunbeam

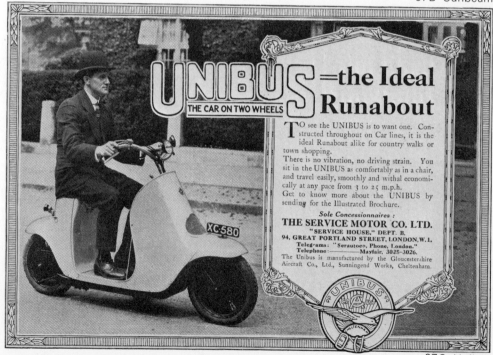

37C Unibus

# THE TWENTIES

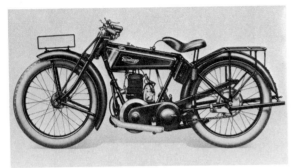

38A Zündapp

38A: Zündapp of Nuremberg first produced motorcycles in 1921 and a few years later introduced a 249-cc two-stroke model which was sold in large numbers. The 1927 model shown featured internal-expanding brakes and proved extremely reliable. Maximum speed was about 75 km/h.

38B: Sidecar combinations were put to various uses, one of them being that of taxicab. This German example plied for hire in the streets of Berlin. Motorcycle taxicabs were employed in several countries, including Great Britain.

38B Sidecar taxicab

38C/D: Leyland Motors of Leyland, Lancashire, based this light first-aid fire-appliance on a BSA V-twin combination. On the fuel tank were both the BSA and the Leyland emblems. It carried a removable Leyland pump unit, powered by its own engine (also a BSA V-twin), and was equipped with many other items of equipment, including lengths of suction and delivery hose. Note the transverse pillion seat for the second crew member. c. 1926.

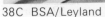

38C BSA/Leyland

38D BSA/Leyland

39A: The military authorities used fairly large numbers of motorcycles and following the successful experiences with double-drive tandem bogies on trucks the British converted some motorcycles to single-track three-wheelers. The specimen shown here was based on a Triumph 'Trusty'. The rearmost wheel was driven by an internal-toothed belt from the chain-drive foremost rear wheel. An overall chain could be fitted over both wheels (*see* the title HALF-TRACKS in this series). A similar machine was built and tested in Germany.

39B: The three-wheeled motorcycle was extensively tested by the RASC in the Aldershot area. It gave a good performance but died a natural death—which was probably as it should have been, for if the terrain is not suitable for a two-wheeled machine it is not likely to be suitable for any machine which depends on balance for its navigation!

39A Triumph

39C Roadless

39B Triumph

39C: Even more ambitious was the tracked motorcycle. This British Roadless model featured a narrow endless rubber track with cable suspension. Turning was by lateral movement of the forward end of the track assembly, by means of steering post 'A'. Powered by a 2¾ HP Douglas flat-twin, it could be driven over meadowland at about 20 mph.

# THE THIRTIES

# Examples of A.J.S 'Perfection in Detail'

On the Big Twin Models the Magdyno is protected by the efficient shield shown here, which ensures reliable ignition even in tropical downpours.

This sketch shows the design of the overhead rocker gear on all the O.H.V. Models. The rockers are duralumin forgings, attached by splines to the hollow alloy steel rocker spindles. Observe the ample diameter of the bronze bushes for the spindles and the neat manner in which the ball-ended duralumin push rods are enclosed.

A well-known feature of A.J.S. Motorcycles is the exceptionally sturdy front fork assembly. Note the accessible finger adjustment for the front brake, the convenient shock absorber adjusting knob, and the stiff headlamp mounting.

FRONT BRAKE ADJUSTMENT

FORK DAMPER ADJUSTMENT

STUDS

SLEEVE BOLTS

SPINDLE and DISTANCE PIECES LOCK NUT

This view shows the simple adjustment for the oil pump provided in the Single-cylinder Models. Also visible are the finger adjustment for the exhaust-valve lifter cable and the very strong front engine mounting.

This cutaway view of the highly efficient front brake used on all Models except 34/12, 34/8 and 34/116 shows the alloy drum with its cooling fins, which serve also to stiffen the drum to prevent distortion, the aluminium alloy brake shoes and the neat manner in which the operating cable is concealed by passing through the front fork tube, whence it emerges at the finger adjuster shown in the illustration.

The arrangement of the "A.J.S." quickly detachable wheel is clearly shown above, the wheel being removable without disturbing the chain or brake. This design is used for front and rear wheels of the Big Twin Models, the wheels being interchangeable and for the rear wheel only of Models 34/6, 34/B8, 34/8, 34/9, 34/7 and 34/10.

"Perfection in detail is the A.J.S. aim" (vide "The Motor Cycle"), and these illustrations show how this "perfection in detail" is attained. The A.J.S. catalogue gives fuller information concerning the refinements on the various A.J.S. models, which range from the 2.48 h.p. "Big Port" to the 9.9 h.p. "Big Twin," and from £40.10.0 to £75. Send the coupon to-day.

Here is the simple and ingenious vernier timing adjustment fitted to all Single-cylinder Models. This gives an extremely fine setting for the magneto timing without the necessity for disturbing any paper fits.

COUPON M.C. 21503

To
A.J.S. Motorcycles,
Plumstead Road,
LONDON, S.E.18.

Please send me the new A.J.S. Catalogue.

Name ........................

Address ........................

40A AJS

40A: The early 'thirties were plagued by the results of the world-wide economic depression and many motorcycle manufacturers went on the rocks, including AJS. However, in 1931 this firm was bought by Matchless, who moved it to London. Production was concentrated on standard touring models but racing machines reappeared a few years later. The advertisement reproduced here dates from March 1934 and highlights some of the design features of the standard production machines.

40B/C: Ariel hit the headlines in 1931 with the introduction of their famous Square Four, which was produced, with continual improvements and modifications, for over twenty years. It had four cylinders with two transverse crankshafts, geared together in their centre, providing superb balance. In 1932 the engine size was increased from 500 to 600 cc (56 × 61 mm) and the following year a wet sump lubrication system replaced the dry sump type with oil tank. The valves were actuated by a single overhead camshaft. Shown is the 1936/37 edition.

40B Ariel

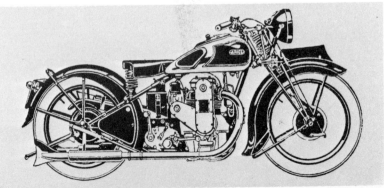

40C Ariel

41A: Benelli of Italy made various types of machines, including this model with gear-drive overhead camshaft. Note the exposed valve springs and flywheel.

41A Benelli

41C BMW

41B BMW

41B: BMW had commenced production of motorcycles in 1923 and used shaft drive from the start. For machines of 500-cc cubic capacity and over the company has always used the transversal flat-twin cylinder configuration; smaller engines, beginning with a 250-cc in 1925, have always had a vertical single cylinder. Illustrated is a 250-cc machine of about 1930.

41C: BMW 750-cc Model R12 (1935—41) with special sidecar fitted out as fire appliance. The twin-cylinder BMWs have always been particularly popular for sidecar work.

41D: The German Army (*Reichswehr* and *Wehrmacht*) during the 'thirties and Second World War employed numerous BMW motorcycles, solo as well as sidecar combinations. This photo shows Hitler and Göring during a drive-past of *Motor-SA* units on the 1935 *Reichs* Party Day.

41D BMW

# THE THIRTIES

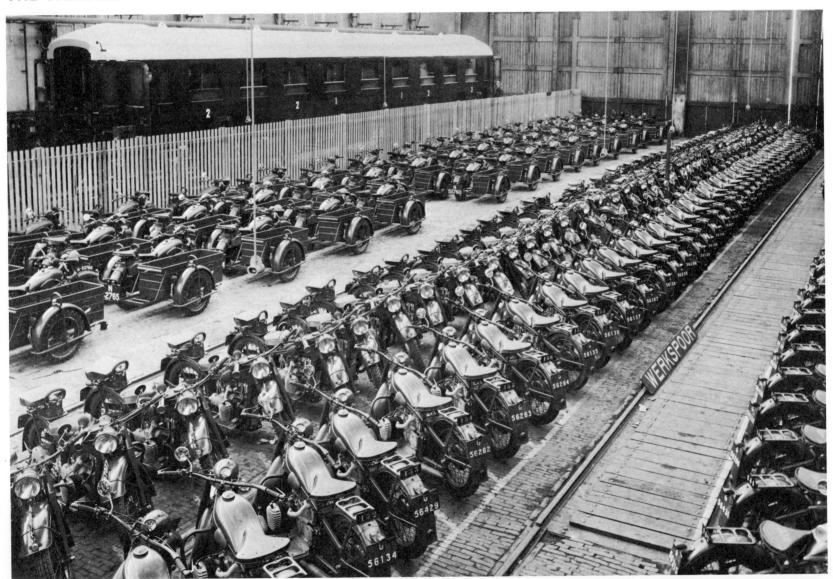

42  BMW and BSA/Werkspoor

42 : Consignment of BMW twins for the Netherlands Army in the works of NV Werkspoor at Utrecht. Here they were fitted with box-type sidecars for use as machine gun carriers and other purposes. At this time, 1938, with anti-German feelings mounting, the Dutch switched over to British BSAs, a number of which are shown in the background ready for delivery. During the last two years before the country was occupied by the Nazis, BSA supplied the Dutch armed forces with more than 1750 600- and 1000-cc motorcycles. Military BSAs were also shipped to South Africa, Eire, India and Sweden, but the bulk of the company's production during 1938—45 was for the British War Office.

43B BSA

43A BMW

43A : Netherlands Army BMW combinations with machine guns during manoeuvres just prior to the Second World War.
43B : In 1932 the British War Office asked BSA to evolve a special 500-cc V-twin-cylinder motorcycle, a type then favoured by the military authorities because of its great flexibility.
43C : The Calthorpe Motor Cycle Co. of Birmingham had been producing OHC models since the late 1920s and in the mid-thirties concentrated on two types of machines : 250- and 500-cc This advertisement appeared in March 1934 and shows the 500-cc model.

43C Calthorpe

# THE THIRTIES

44A CZ

44A: CZ was, and still is, one of Czechoslovakia's leading motorcycle makes. The initials stood for Ceska Zbrojovka (Czech Armaments factory) and the firm is based in Strakonice. During 1933—37 about 5000 of these CZ 100 lightweights were produced. The power unit was a small 98-cc (50 × 50 mm) two-stroke, developing 2 HP at 2000 rpm and started by turning the pedals with the (multi-disc) clutch kept disengaged. The machine weighed 45 kg and had a maximum speed of about 40 km/h.

44D FN

44B: The German DKW company produced large numbers of two-stroke motorcycles for customers all over the world. In 1932 DKW became part of the new Auto Union AG, a combine which also included the motorcar manufacturers Horch, Wanderer and Audi. By this time DKW had also started production of front-wheel drive cars with transversally-mounted water-cooled two-stroke engines. A similar engine was used in the motorcycle shown here, a 498-cc model of 1933.

44B DKW

44C Douglas

44C: Derived from the well-known Douglas horizontally-opposed twin-cylinder motorcycle engine was the water-cooled power unit of this generating set. During the Second World War Douglas produced generating sets for the British Army.

44D: In 1937 the Belgian FN company produced this impressive Model M14 sidecar racing combination. The engine was a 500-cc transverse twin with overhead camshaft and compressor. Tyre size was 3.00-21 front, 3.25-20 rear (27 × 3 and 27 × 3.25 resp.)

45A: During the late 1930s the Belgian manufacturers FN, Gillet and Sarolea (*q.v.*) produced military motorcycle combinations with sidecar wheel drive. Illustrated is the 1937–39 FN Model M12, which had a 1000-cc side-valve flat-twin air-cooled engine. Many of these machines fell into German hands during 1940 and were subsequently used by the *Wehrmacht* (shown).

45A FN

45B Francis-Barnett

45B: Francis-Barnett Cruiser, Model J45, of Sept. 1939. This well-preserved specimen, powered by a 249-cc Villiers Type XVIIIa two-stroke engine, has been in daily use by Mr Eric S. Beale of Redhill, Surrey, since the war years and so far has clocked up over 111,000 miles. Noteworthy are the deep mudguards and the contoured shields protecting engine and transmission.

45C: In 1937 the Italian Pierro Taruffi broke several speed records in this mighty Gilera 500-cc 4-cyl. with compressor. On the *autostrada* Bergamo-Brescia he attained 274 km/h. . . .

45D: Belgian Gillet 750 sidecar combination of 1938, produced for the *Gendarmerie* (and, with slightly different specification, for the Army). The power unit was a two-stroke transverse twin, driving the rear and sidecar wheel through a gearbox with four forward speeds and one reverse. This machine has been preserved in Belgium.

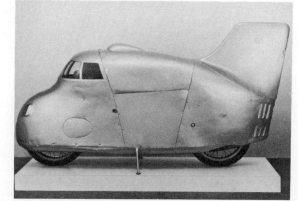

45C Gilera

45D Gillet

# THE THIRTIES

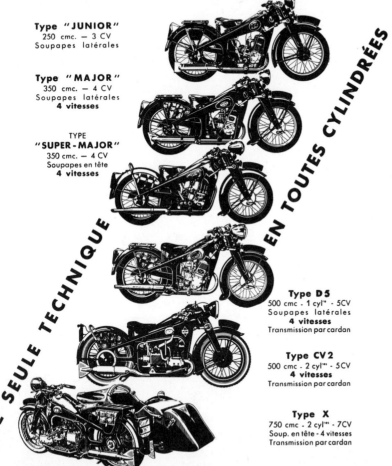

## GNOME·RHONE

UNE SEULE TECHNIQUE EN TOUTES CYLINDRÉES

**Type "JUNIOR"**
250 cmc. — 3 CV
Soupapes latérales

**Type "MAJOR"**
350 cmc. — 4 CV
Soupapes latérales
**4 vitesses**

TYPE
**"SUPER-MAJOR"**
350 cmc. — 4 CV
Soupapes en tête
**4 vitesses**

**Type D 5**
500 cmc - 1 cyl* - 5CV
Soupapes latérales
**4 vitesses**
Transmission par cardan

**Type CV 2**
500 cmc - 2 cyl** - 5CV
**4 vitesses**
Transmission par cardan

**Type X**
750 cmc - 2 cyl** - 7CV
Soup. en tête - 4 vitesses
Transmission par cardan

**SIÈGE SOCIAL:** 150, Boul. Haussmann, PARIS-8° - **VENTE:** 49, Avenue de la Grande-Armée. — **SUCCURSALES:** LILLE, 140, Rue Nationale. — LYON, 25, Avenue Jean Jaurès. — MARSEILLE, 185 bis, Rue de Rome. — NANCY, 5, Rue St-Julien. — TOULOUSE, 6, Rue d'Aubuisson. — ALGER, 41, Rue Sadi Carnot.

46A Gnome-Rhône

46A: The French Gnome-Rhône production programme in 1938—top to bottom: Junior (3 HP, 250 cc, side valves), Major (4 HP, 350 cc, side valves, four speeds), Super-Major (4 HP, 350 cc, OHV, four speeds), D5 (5 HP, 500 cc, side valves, four speeds, shaft drive), CV2 (5 HP, 500 cc, OHV, two opposed cylinders, four speeds, shaft drive), X (7 HP, 750 cc, OHV, two opposed cylinders, four speeds, shaft drive). Of the latter there was a military version, called the 750 *Armée*; a heavier military model with 804-cc engine and sidecar wheel drive, designated Model AX2, was also made. All models featured a pressed-steel frame.

46B: Italian Moto Guzzi Alce *Monoposto* as used by the Italian armed forces from 1939. It had a 500-cc horizontal single-cylinder engine of 13.2 HP with exposed flywheel and four-speed gearbox. Tyre size was 3.50-19, maximum speed 90 km/h, weight 180 kg. The machine had a 'sprung frame', i.e. the rear wheel was mounted in hinged trailing-type forks. Some had a pillion seat (*Biposto*).

46B Moto Guzzi

47: The Moto Guzzi military Model GT17 was introduced in 1932 and had basically the same engine as the Alce (46B) albeit with a three-speed gearbox. It is shown in *Biposto* form but was used also as *Monoposto* (i.e. without pillion seat). A derivative was the GT17 *Mototriciclo Militare 32*—a motortricycle with truck-type body capable of carrying a payload of 300 kg. Maximum speeds were 100 and 53 km/h respectively.

47  Moto Guzzi

# THE THIRTIES

48A Moto Guzzi

48A: In 1933 Moto Guzzi developed a racing machine with an engine combining two of their 250-cc (68 × 68 mm) cylinders in 120° V-formation. Each cylinder had a single overhead camshaft, driven by a train of bevel gears, and the power output ranged from 44 HP at 7000 rpm to 52 at 8000, giving top speeds from 170 to 210 km/h (106–131 mph). The gearbox had four speeds and the machine weighed about 160 kg. Moto Guzzis of this type (2C) won many races, including the Monza Grand Prix in 1934, 1935 and 1936, the British TT in 1935, the Swiss Grand Prix in 1951 and six Italian Championship Titles during the period 1934 to 1949.

48B Moto Guzzi

48B: This was the first multi-cylinder racing engine designed by Moto Guzzi, in 1930: a trans-versely-mounted four-in-line (56 × 50 mm, 492 cc) with supercharger. It developed 45 HP at 7800 rpm and had three speeds. Top speed was 175 km/h. In the words of the manufacturers 'this engine, however, developed too much power for those days and this proved a negative factor as it could never be completely subdued'. The machine, designated 4C, was never raced.

48C Harley-Davidson

48D Harley-Davidson

48C: Harley-Davidson motorcycles formed a class of their own and were very popular with police forces all over the world. These machines were in service with the Brazilian Presidential Guards.

48D: The US Army also invested heavily in Harley-Davidsons, employing them for various purposes, including reconnaissance, messenger service, convoy and traffic control, etc. Shown is a motorcycle scout, equipped with a short-wave radio for reporting reconnaissance details back to his operations base.

49A Indian

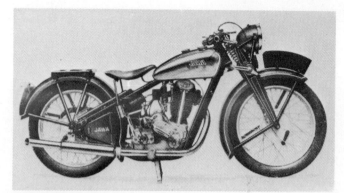

49C: Jawa in Czechoslovakia, which still has a name of high repute in the motorcycle industry, in 1937 produced various types of machines, including this little pedal-assist 100-cc model.

49D Jawa

49A: Indian was Harley-Davidson's chief competitor in the USA and their V-twin did not look much unlike the Harley. Main exterior distinguishing features, apart from the name on the tank, were the opposite locations of the gearshift lever (RH side on the Indian) and the front forks which on the Indian incorporated a quarter-elliptic laminated leaf spring. Shown is the Indian Chief, a 1200-cc V-twin, in its mid-thirties guise.

49B: The Indian Motorcycle Co. also produced a four-cylinder in-line model, the Indian Four. It was a heavy machine, weighing about 250 kg. The engine cubic capacity was near-enough 1300 cc. Another US manufacturer of four-in-line motorcycles was Henderson (see 32A).

49D: A heavier Jawa, also of 1937, was the 350-cc OHV model shown here. During this year Jawa produced about 30,000 motorcycles for domestic use and export.

49C Jawa

49E: Another Czech marque was the lesser-known Koch of which the 350-cc model of 1935 is illustrated. Noteworthy are the modern lines with very deep mudguards and telescopic front forks. The OHV single-cylinder (74·5 × 80 mm) engine was good for 115 km/h. The machine weighed just under 140 kg.

49B Indian

49E Koch

# THE THIRTIES

50A PMZ

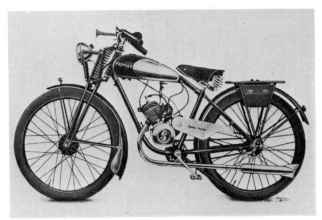

50B Premier

50C Promet

50A: The Russians made various types of motorcycles, including this Indian-inspired PMZ A-750, a 100-km/h V-twin of 747-cc (70 × 97 mm) and 14 HP at 3700 rpm. It had a three-speed gearbox and a pressed-steel frame. Tyre size was 4.50–18, weight about 220 kg. It was also used with sidecar. 1935–36.

50B: The Premier was made by a company which was originally (1912–13) based in Nuremberg, as the German branch of the British Premier works of Coventry, but which in 1913 had been moved across the nearby border to the Austro-Hungarian territory which in 1918 became Czechoslovakia. There the Premier was produced until the mid-1930s. This pedal-assist lightweight had a German 100-cc Fichtel & Sachs engine.

50D Puch

50C: This unusual rear-engined machine was produced in 1936 by the Soviet Promet motorcycle works in Leningrad. The 2-HP two-stroke engine drove the rear wheel directly, without clutch or gearbox. Having no pedals it had to be push-started; stopping was accomplished by means of a decompression lever. The machine, which had large-section tyres and no springs, was claimed to be good for 70 km/h.

50D: Another 'motorized bicycle' from central Europe was this Austrian 1·5-HP Puch Model 60. It was in production during 1937–38 and had a 60·3-cc (40 × 48 mm) two-stroke engine with the crankshaft placed longitudinally and single-speed transmission. It weighed 39 kg and had a top speed of around 30 km/h.

50E: A larger Puch of the same period was the Model 200, which had a pressed-steel frame and a 6-HP dual-piston 198-cc (2 × 45 × 62·8 mm) two-stroke power unit with four-speed gearbox. This model, too, had a transversal engine. It topped about 75 km/h and weighed just over 100 kg.

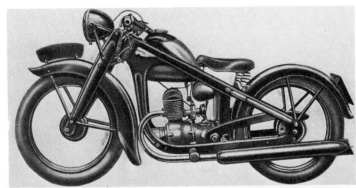

50E Puch

51A : Biggest Puchs of the early thirties were the Models 500 ZNN, V and VL, powered by a 489-cc two-stroke twin with four pistons (2 × 2 × 45 × 78 mm), developing 14 HP at 3600 rpm. They were excellently suited for sidecar combinations, an example of which is shown. In 1936 Puch introduced a heavy four-cylinder four-stroke 792-cc 20-HP machine, the 800, which in solo form could reach 125 km/h.

51B : This 496-cc side-valve Raleigh of 1930 was displayed in entirely original—unrestored—condition at the Historic Transport Rally in Ardingly, Sussex, in July 1974. It was made in Nottingham.

51C/D : In addition to the Gnome-Rhône military sidecar combinations (*see* 46A) the French Army used machines of several other makes, including René Gillet. These were made by René Gillet of Montrouge (Seine) and should not be confused with the Gillet (*q.v.*) made in Herstal, Belgium. The French armed forces used sidecars for various roles and shown here are two different types, both carrying a machine gun. Some were equipped with armour plating. An all-enclosed radio-communications sidecar also existed.

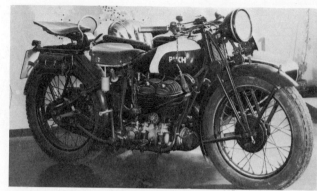

51A  Puch

51B  Raleigh

51E : The Japanese Imperial Army used heavy motor-cycles, solo and with sidecar, which were clearly replicas of the Harley-Davidson. This combination, known as the Sankyo Type 97 (1937), had a 24-HP 1196-cc V-twin-cylinder engine with three-speed gearbox and turned the scales at about 500 kg (280 without sidecar).

51C  René Gillet

51D  René Gillet

51E  Sankyo

# THE THIRTIES

52A Sarolea

52B : A beautifully preserved Triumph Tiger 100 of 1938/39, on display at a rally in England 35 years later. This model was based on Triumph's famous Speed Twin and replaced their 1938 Tiger 90 model.

52B Triumph

52A : Sarolea, like FN, Gillet and Gnome-Rhône, during the late 'thirties produced heavy military motorcycle/sidecar combinations with two-wheel drive. It is believed that some of the above firms continued production of these machines for some time under the German occupation; the Germans themselves began making similar machines in 1940 (BMW, Zündapp). Shown is a trio of Saroleas, equipped with wireless transmitting and receiving sets. These machines had a 978-cc (88 × 80 mm) horizontally-opposed air-cooled side-valve engine, a gearbox with three forward speeds and one reverse plus an auxiliary reduction gear set of the planetary type, providing a total of six forward and two reverse ratios. Maximum speed was just over 80 km/h.

52C : The Vincent-HRD was first conceived in the 1920s when Howard R. Davies won the 1925 Senior TT on a machine of his own design, the HRD. It was later fitted with a Vincent spring frame and as the Vincent-HRD became one of Britain's most famous marques, surviving until well after the Second World War. The advertisement reproduced here appeared in March 1934 when the firm offered a water-cooled 250 and an OHV 500, both with spring frame and semi-enclosed.

52D : A widely-used machine of the German *Wehrmacht* was the Zündapp KS 600, produced during 1937–40. Other heavy Zündapp combinations used by Hitler's armed forces were the 500-cc K500 (1934–39) and the 800-cc K800. BMW supplied the 750-cc R12 (1935–41), NSU the 600-cc 601OSL (1938–39). The sidecars were usually of the *Einheits* (standardized) type. Lighter models were made by BMW, DKW, NSU, Triumph (TWN), Victoria, etc.

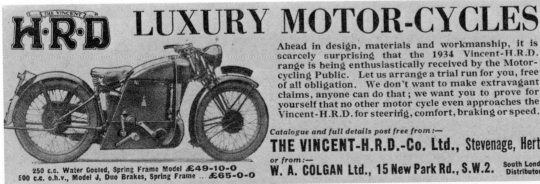

52C Vincent-HRD

52D Zündapp

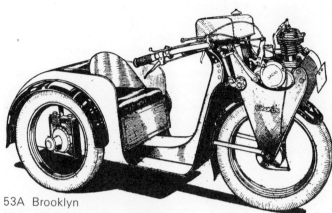

53A Brooklyn

53A : Three-wheelers or tricars
as passenger-carrying vehicles were
not built in large numbers during the 'thirties,
the main exception being the single-rear-wheel British
Morgan. This French 'trike', called the Snowden, was
introduced by the French Brooklyn firm in 1934. The power
unit, mounted above the front wheel, was a German 100-cc
Sachs two-stroke with two-speed gearbox built in unit,
gear changing being effected by a lever mounted on the
handlebars. Many steel pressings were used in the bodywork and independently sprung wheels were another
feature. Maximum speed was 34 mph and it was claimed
to have averaged 20 mph for 26 hours during a
rigorous road test.

53E Toyo Kogyo

53B : General Motors' Delco
Appliance Division in the USA in
1938/39 designed and built a
military motortricycle for the US
Army. It had a car-type rear axle and
followed European heavy motorcycle
design in having a horizontally-
opposed transverse twin-cylinder
engine with shaft drive. The project
remained experimental.

53C : FN Tricar of 1939 was a military
multi-purpose machine, derived
from the company's M12 motorcycle
(q.v.). It could carry 600 kg or five
people.

53D : Indian and Harley-Davidson
in the USA both offered three-
wheelers, derived from their conventional motorcycles. Shown is an
Indian military model. At the rear
there was a locker, with a seat for
two passengers. Such machines
were popular with garages as
service vehicles and often had a
towing attachment at the front
which could be hitched to the
rear bumper of a car. They were
also used by the police.

53E : Toyo Kogyo (now better
known as Mazda) and several other
Japanese manufacturers during the
'thirties produced considerable
numbers of *Sanrinsha* (motortricycle)
light trucks. Shown is the Toyo
Kogyo Model DA, some of which
were reputedly exported to China.
The Japanese also based light fire
appliances and other vehicles on
this type of chassis.

53B Delco

53C FN

53D Indian

# THE SECOND WORLD WAR

54A : In Britain the production of civilian motorcycles virtually ceased on the outbreak of the Second World War and the same applied in most if not all of the other belligerent nations. Selected manufacturers received considerable orders for military machines, usually sturdy and straightforward derivatives from civilian models. Britain in particular had requirements for large numbers of motorcycles, especially after the heavy losses at Dunkirk. As in the First World War many thousands of suitable civilian machines were impressed. Shown is a string of Ariel W/NG 350-cc machines, used for the training of freshly-recruited dispatch-riders.

54A Ariel

54B : BMW and Zündapp in 1940 started production of special purpose-built military sidecar combinations, designated R75 and KS750 respectively, for the German *Wehrmacht*. Both had 750-cc horizontally-opposed two-cylinder engines and sidecar wheel drive through a lockable differential. The general configuration was similar to the Belgian French machines shown and mentioned in previous pages and of which considerable numbers were captured by the Germans in 1939/40. Shown are surviving examples of both the BMW and Zündapp, owned by Mr Tony L. Oliver in England. (*See* also Fig. 60E.)

54C : BSA was one of the main British suppliers of military motorcycles during the 1939—45 war, delivering 126,334 units out of the total of some 425,000 supplied to the War Office by British manufacturers. Both 350- and 500-cc models were made, with overhead and side valves respectively. Shown is one of the latter (Model M20), alongside a Humber Light Reconnaissance car. BSA, as well as Matchless and Velocette and other British machines, were also supplied to Russia, under the Lend-Lease agreement.

54B BMW

54C BSA

# THE SECOND WORLD WAR

55A : The Cushman Motor Works of Lincoln, Nebraska, supplied the US armed forces with various types of motorscooters, namely an airborne solo type (Model 53), a sidecar combination (Model 34) and a three-wheeler 'Package Car' (Model 39) with two wheels at front. All had a single-cylinder four-stroke engine with two-speed gearbox. The airborne type (shown) featured parachute-attaching rings and a small pintle hook at the rear.

55A Cushman

55B : DKW Model NZ350 was procured by the German *Wehrmacht* in large numbers. A very reliable and rugged machine, it had a single-cylinder 346-cc (72 × 85 mm) two-stroke engine with a maximum output of 11 HP at 4000 rpm. Maximum speed was about 100 km/h. From 1944 till war's end all German military motorcycle production consisted of DKW 125-cc (RT) and 350-cc machines.

55C : The British for airborne use developed the 'Welbike' parascooter. It had a 98-cc Excelsior two-stroke engine with single-speed transmission (after the war it was produced by Brockhouse, with two-speed gearbox and called Corgie). This parascooter had collapsible steering etc. and was parachuted in a special container, as shown. The Italians had a somewhat similar scooter, the Volugrafo Aermoto, which had a 125-cc engine with two-speed gearbox plus double-reduction gear for pulling heavy loads.

55B DKW

55C Excelsior 'Welbike'

55D Gilera

55D : In addition to the Moto Guzzi (*see* page 48) the Italian forces during the Second World War employed several other makes of 500-cc motorcycles, including the (Moto) Gilera, shown here in *Biposto* form. It had a single-cylinder side-valve engine and, like the Guzzi, a sprung frame.

# THE SECOND WORLD WAR

56A Harley-Davidson

56B Harley-Davidson

56A: Harley-Davidson during the 1939—45 period supplied tens of thousands of motorcycles, chiefly the 45 cubic inch model, to the American and allied forces. Shown is a line-up of 45WLAs of the US Armored Division, delivered before the country got directly involved in the war itself. Note the front fork-mounted holders for the sub-machine guns.

56B: Main wartime customers of Harley-Davidson outside the USA were Britain and Canada. This smart WL of the Royal Air Force Police was photographed during the big Victory Parade in London on 8 June 1946. American motorcycles used by the RAF during the war were almost exclusively Indians, in addition to the British Ariel, BSA, Matchless, Norton, Royal Enfield, Triumph and Velocette.

56C: For the Canadian armed forces Harley-Davidson produced a variant of the 45WLA, designated 45WLC. One is shown here in a school for Canadian MT (Motor Transport) mechanics, operated in Britain during the early part of the war.

56C Harley-Davidson

57A: Typical Indian combination as used by the US forces in 1940–41. This type of machine was subsequently superseded by the famous 'Jeep' cross-country car. Some experimental ultra-light field cars produced in the USA in 1943 were powered by engines of Harley-Davidson and Indian make and both manufacturers produced limited numbers of— for them—unusual motorcycles, with transverse twin engines and shaft drive (see The Observer's Fighting Vehicles Directory— World War II for these and other additional military two- and three-wheeled motorcycles).

57B: The James ML 'Clockwork Mouse' was one of two British military motorcycles with a 125-cc engine (Villiers two-stroke, 50 × 62 mm, 3·2 HP at 3800 rpm). It weighed 139 lb dry, 157 lb with the tank full, and had a three-speed gearbox. Handlebars and footrests could be folded, thus decreasing the overall width to 1 ft 4 in. This machine has been preserved and restored in England. The other lightweight was the Royal Enfield RE 125 'Flying Flea', virtually a replica of the German DKW RT.

57C: The Soviet heavy sidecar combination produced from 1942 was known plainly as the M-72. It was patterned on the German BMW R71 and had a horizontal twin-cylinder engine of 746 cc (78 × 78 mm) producing 22 HP at 4500 rpm, 4-speed gearbox and shaft drive. It was used also as a solo machine, the kerb weights being 335 and 205 kg respectively.

57B James

57C M-72

57D Matchless

57E MCB/Nymanbolagen (NV)

57D: Matchless' masterpiece in the Second World War was the sprightly G3/L, a 350 OHV machine with telescopic hydraulic ('teledraulic') front forks, good ground clearance, reasonably low weight and other attractive features. After the war it remained in production with but few modifications.

57E: The Swedes, too, produced a big twin with shaft drive to rear and sidecar wheel; this machine was introduced in 1943 by Nymanbolagen (NV) and featured a 1000-cc V-2-cylinder engine with six forward gears and reverse. The Monark m/42, a single-cylinder 500-cc model, was more numerous, however. Both makes were part of the MCB group.

57A Indian

# THE SECOND WORLD WAR

58A Norton

58B Royal Enfield

58A: Norton Motors Ltd produced over 100,000 military motorcycles, both for the British and the Canadians. They were the only British manufacturers to make a sidecar combination with two-wheel drive (Model 633 'Big Four'). Their other military machine was the rugged 16H, used solo and with conventional sidecar. The two had single-cylinder side-valve engines of 633- and 496-cc cubic capacity respectively; examples of both types are illustrated.

58B: Royal Enfield 350-cc WD machines were the mounts of these two (of many) ATS drivers: Sergeant Margery Baggott of Margate (right) and Corporal Joyce Parkis of Church Stretton. The Commer 3-ton GS trucks in the background, loaded with ammunition, were also driven by girls of the ATS—the Auxiliary Territorial Service, which later became the WRAC.

58C: The Simplex Servi-Cycle was an unusual American machine, produced by the Simplex Manufacturing Co. of New Orleans for airborne purposes. It was used by, among others, the Canadian Army in England. The power unit was a small two-stroke with twin spark plugs and flywheel-magneto ignition. The most unusual feature was that both primary and secondary drive were not by chain but by V-belt, making it one of the last machines to use this old-fashioned system. Instead of the usual twist grip, the throttle was operated by what normally is the clutch handle; the clutch control itself was a pedal on the left-hand side which, when pushed in, caused the drive pulley to slip within the final drive belt. There were no gearbox and kick-starter.

58C Simplex

59: Large consignment of Triumph motorcycles, ready for issue at a Royal Army Service Corps depot in December 1939. Triumph supplied 350-cc models of side-valve (Model 3SW, shown) and OHV (Model 3HW) design.

59 Triumph

# THE SECOND WORLD WAR

60A Velocette

60A : Veloce's wartime military motorcycle was the
Velocette 350-cc OHV Model MAF, many thousands
of which were supplied to the War Office. It was
developed from the civilian Model MAC. The Soviet
Union received a number of Velocettes under Lend-
Lease.

60B : Zündapp single-cylinder two-stroke machine,
one of many pre-1939 models used by the German
Army in the *Blitzkrieg*. In the background are
Cologne-built Ford 3-ton trucks.
60C : Typical wartime advertisement : 'Zündapp—
reliable on all fronts'. Until 1940 this Nuremberg
(later Munich) firm supplied conventional twin-
cylinder models to the German armed forces (*see*
page 52).
60D/E : During 1940–44 Zündapp, as well as BMW
(*q.v.*), produced purpose-built heavy military sidecar
combinations. The two firms reputedly delivered
16,500 and 18,635 units respectively. Of these, only
a few have survived and a restored specimen is
shown in Fig. 60E. The Zündapp, Model KS750,
had a 751-cc (75 × 85 mm) OHV opposed-twin
engine, developing 26 HP at 4000 rpm. The BMW
had the same power output but 78 mm bore and
stroke (746 cc). Both had 4.50/4.75-16 tyres and
hydraulic brakes on the rear and sidecar wheels ;
the front brake was cable-operated. In addition
to its four forward speeds the Zündapp had a
reverse gear (as did the BMW) and an extra-low
ratio for cross-country work. The sidecar was of
standardized type.

60B Zündapp

ZÜNDAPP
zuverlässig
an allen Fronten

ZÜNDAPP-WERKE G.M.B.H. NÜRNBERG

60C Zündapp

60D Zündapp

60E Zündapp

61A  Benelli

61C  Moto Guzzi

61A: Benelli in Italy produced solo machines (250- and 500-cc) as well as motortricycles for the Italian armed forces. One of the latter is shown. It had a 500-cc single-cylinder engine and a truck-type box body, suspended on long semi-elliptic leaf springs.

61B: Moto Guzzi was probably Italy's largest producer of military motortricycles. This is a Trialce *mototriciclo smontabile* with folding frame and horizontal 13·2-HP 500-cc engine, made in 1942 and derived from the Alce solo machine (*see* 46B).

61C: Heavy Moto Guzzi Model 500U, used as a mobile gun mount (*motocarro porta mitragliera*). This vehicle, built in 1942, was much heavier than the Trialce and had a 17·8-HP 500-cc power unit, with four-speed gearbox. Wheelbase was 2·30 m, track 1·30 m, The disc wheels were shod with 6.00-16 tyres and the vehicle's carrying capacity was 1000 kg. Maximum speed was given as 67 km/h. It was more common as a general service load carrier.

61B  Moto Guzzi

# THE SECOND WORLD WAR

62A NSU

62A: One of the most unusual 'motorcycles' to emerge from the Second World War was the NSU HK101 *Kettenkraftrad*, more commonly known as the *Kettenkrad* (*Krad* was short for *Kraftrad*—German for motorcycle; *Ketten* means tracks). It was made during 1941–44 by NSU and in 1943 also by Stoewer of Stettin. Altogether some 8345 were delivered to the *Wehrmacht*, who designated it *Sd.Kfz.2*. It probably first saw active service in the airborne invasion of Crete in 1942.

62B: The *Kettenkrad* was an ingenious, albeit complicated, machine, with the same track bogie construction as the heavier German semi-track vehicles in the 1- to 18-ton classes. The tracks were propelled by a back-to-front Opel Olympia 1·5-litre OHV four-cylinder car engine, driving through a three-speed gearbox with high and low range. Steering was accomplished by turning the handlebars in the normal fashion but for sharp turns this actuated the controlled differential, providing skid steering. A larger model—HK102 *Grosser Kettenkraftrad*—with a 2-litre engine was also developed, but not produced in quantity.

62C: This NSU *Kettenkrad* was one of several hundred which survived the war; it found its way to Mürzzuschlag in Austria where it was employed by the Fire Service as a light fire appliance for mountainous areas.

62C NSU

62D: Another survivor, although hardly recognizable as such, was this machine, consisting of a modified *Kettenkrad* with a *c.* 1950 Volkswagen car front end—an ambitious and painstaking project, resulting in a most interesting 'marriage'. It was seen in the Cologne area in the mid-1960s.

62D NSU/Volkswagen

63B

63A–D : The German *Wehrmacht* used very large numbers of motorcycles during the war and experienced plenty of difficulties in the muds and sands of Russia and North Africa. Like the Americans, for tactical use the Germans gradually replaced their sidecar combinations by four-wheeled cross-country cars, the 'Jeep' and the VW 'Kübel' respectively.

63C

63D

# INDEX

Abingdon 26
AC (Autocarrier) 15, 26
Adria 27
AJS 26–28, 40
Ariel 26, 28, 40, 54, 56

BAT 26
BD 28, 35
Beeston 6
Benelli 41, 61
Bianchi 19
BMW 41–43, 52, 54, 57, 60
Bradbury 26
Brennabor 26
Brooklyn 53
Brough 28
BSA 15, 17, 26, 29, 38, 42, 43, 54, 56
Burney & Blackburne 26
Butler 4

Calthorpe 26, 43
Campion 26
Cechie-Böhmerland 29
Centaur 26
Clyno 21, 26
Copeland 4
Cushman 55
CZ 44

Daimler 4
De Dion-Bouton 6
Delco 53
DKW 29, 30, 44, 52, 55
Douglas 16, 22–26, 30, 39, 44

Esse 31
Excelsior 12, 13, 55
Eysink 15, 18

Fafnir 10
FN 10, 11, 26, 31, 44, 53
Francis-Barnett 45
Frera 19

Gilera 45, 55
Gillet 45

Gnome-Rhône 46
Griffon 26
Guzzi 32, 46–48, 61

Harley-Davidson 3, 20, 21, 26, 48, 53, 56, 57
Henderson 32
Hercules 10
Hildebrand & Wolfmüller 5
Humber 6, 7, 14, 26

Imperial 26
Indian 19, 21, 26, 32, 49, 53, 57

James 26, 57
JAP 11, 26
Jawa 49

Koch 49

Laurin & Klement 7, 10
Lea-Francis 26
Levis 26
Leyland 38
Leon Bollée 5
LMC 26

M-72 57
Magnet 26
Matchless 26, 54, 56, 57
MCB 57
Merryweather 4, 14
Michaux 4
Millet 5
Minerva 13
Monark 31, 33, 57
(Moto) Gilera 45, 55
(Moto) Guzzi 32, 46–48, 61
Motosacoche 10, 26

Ner-a-Car 33
New Hudson 26, 30
New Imperial 26, 33
Norton 26, 34, 56, 58
NSU 26, 52, 62
NUT 11, 26, 34
NV 34, 57

OEC 34
OK Junior 26

Perks and Birch 8
Phelon & Moore (Panther) 7, 24, 26
PMZ 50
Praga 35
Premier 26, 50
Promet 50
Puch 35, 36, 50, 51

Quadrant 26

Raleigh 30, 51
Regal 26
René Gillet 51
Rex 13, 26
Roadless 39
Rover 26
Royal Enfield 10, 21, 26, 36, 56–58
Royal Ruby 26
Rudge (-Whitworth) 26, 36

Sankyo 51
Sarolea 52
Scott 11, 21, 26, 37
Sheffield-Simplex 33
Simplex 58
Singer 8, 9, 13, 26
Snowden 53
Sparkbrook 26
Sun 26
Sunbeam 26, 30, 37

Toyo Kogyo 53
Triumph 11, 14, 17, 23, 24–26, 39, 52, 56, 58, 59
Triumph (TWN) 52

Unibus 37

Velocette 54, 56, 60
Victoria 52
Vincent-HRD 52
Volugrafo 55

Wall 15
Wanderer 26
Warwick 26
Welbike 55
Werner 5

Zenith 26
Zündapp 38, 52, 54, 60

## ACKNOWLEDGEMENTS

This book was compiled and written largely from historic source material in the library of the Olyslager Organisation, and in addition photographs and information were provided by several manufacturers and individuals, notably Messrs E. S. Beale, W. F. Buskell, J. Herink, A. van Ingelgom, A. Krenn, C. Lake and B. H. Vanderveen.